# Mother of Inmates

Teresa Tarpley

*with Lisa Bell*

*This book is dedicated to all mothers of inmates who don't know where to turn or who to trust. To those with hearts that repeatedly ache from constantly seeing your children in jail or prison. Today, I'm here to let you know the way to cope with the many emotions. His name is Jesus.*

*"And I will give you the keys of the kingdom of heaven, and whatever you bind on earth will be bound in heaven, and whatever you loose on earth will be loosed in heaven." (Matthew 16:19 NKJV)*

# Contents

*Acknowledgments*............................................................vii

*Introduction*....................................................................1

*Chapter 1 ~  I Liked Men* ...............................................3

*Chapter 2 ~  Negative Heard—Negative Learned*.....7

*Chapter 3 ~  I Didn't Realize* .......................................14

*Chapter 4 ~  My Big Boy*..............................................20

*Chapter 5 ~  My Baby Boy* ...........................................29

*Chapter 6 ~  Parents, Check Yourself.*.......................37

*Chapter 7 ~  Then and Now* .......................................49

*About the Author*...........................................................58

*About Radical Women*...................................................60

*Other Books by Teresa Tarpley*...................................61

"Therefore, I say to you, whatever things you ask when you pray, believe that you receive them, and you will have them."
(Mark 11:24)

# *Acknowledgments*

Above all, I thank and honor the Father, Son and Holy Spirit for teaching me throughout the trials of my life—the mental and physical addictions and trials I endured made me the woman I am today with a heart that desires nothing more than helping others.

I also thank God for exposing me to myself and teaching me how not only to forgive others, but to forgive myself. Through the painful challenges of my life, I learned and now I can share my testimony with others going through tough times as well.

Thank you, God, for allowing all my hurt to be a testimony for someone else.

I pray God uses the words in this short book to comfort and guide other parents with incarcerated children. May He use this book to draw our children to Him.

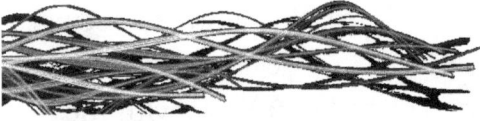

*"Those who do not know emotional baggage also do not know about the tribulations of the world.*
*But those who do not learn to cope with its burdens also forget about its beauty."*
— *Dahi Tamara Koch*

# *Introduction*

Having one child in jail or juvenile detention causes a headache. Two in jail? At the same time? That's double trouble, and enough to take most mothers down for the count. Not only for mothers, I wouldn't wish this on any person—not even my worst enemy.

As the mother of four children, I hoped none of them got into trouble with the law, but two did. Before they reached their teenage years, I already knew the agony of seeing your babies in jail.

Only two stayed in trouble with the police. I should feel blessed that half my children stayed clean, and I am. That doesn't lessen emotions from dealing with the other two.

Whether they were cutting class or disrupting the class, I often took time off from my job to attend juvenile court. Frustrated, I went, knowing every time meant losing money if I left work, yet believing I needed to be there for them and pray God changed their hearts.

I won't say I didn't play a part in all this. Sometimes we do the best we know how to do at the time. I copied the way others raised their children, never realizing I didn't truly know the people I imitated or if they knew the right way to raise a child. My role models didn't give me the greatest pattern either.

As I dealt with having sons in jail or prison, I learned from my mistakes and theirs. I pray, now, that by sharing my story and insights, perhaps I can help another through this trying time as a *Mother of Inmates*.

*"Forgiveness is really about absolution: to set free. But if you look carefully at the dynamic, the one you're setting free is yourself."*

— *Darrell Calkins*

# Chapter 1 ~
# I Liked Men

I spent a great deal of time around men most of my life, always liking them—still do. But I don't always like the things some of them do.

Throughout life, I tried liking and dating guys with nine-to-five jobs. I wanted to like those men. For some unknown, crazy reason, that never was good enough for me. Drawn to the hardcore, pimps, thugs, players, drug dealers and ex-offenders, I went after them. Maybe they came after me, and I responded.

People always said, "Get with a dude fresh out of prison. They perform the best sex."

That made sense, and the old Teresa liked that idea a lot. If you want a temporary good time, go for it. Unfortunately, sex doesn't equal love, and those men don't stick around too long.

Others told me, "Be there when a man gets released from jail or prison. Help him get up on his feet by giving him money, buying him shoes, clothes, cars. Put him back in his street game, and he'll be with you forever."

How I wanted to believe these people knew what they said. So, I tried both these methods, often with the same man. Yes, back then I liked it.

> "Insanity is doing the same thing over and over again and expecting different results."
>
> Albert Einstein

These people didn't know squat about life. Every man I got with fresh out of prison didn't stick around. Each time, he got all he wanted from me. Then suddenly he disappeared. I didn't see him for a long while.

Soon after I started wondering where that man went, I'd learn he went back to jail or prison. Because I had no self-respect, I'd say, "Oh well, I'll holla when he hit the streets."

One time didn't teach me anything. I continued the same attempt at catching a man repeatedly, always ending up with the same results. The great genius Albert Einstein said, "Insanity is doing the same thing over and over again and expecting different results."

Maybe I had a little insanity going on back before I knew the truth of Jesus Christ. For sure, I had more than enough addictions and generational curses running through my veins.

Looking back, I thank God for ridding my life of men who had no business getting near me. So many men walked away from me, and I honestly am thankful. I didn't know it at the time, but God spared me more heartache caused by staying with some of these unsavory characters.

Yes, the rejection hurt—sometimes more than words can express. All of it together affected more than me. I had young children. When we have kids, we do nothing that doesn't leave a mark on their lives, good or bad.

Ironically, I didn't end up in prison, although I probably should have many times. God's grace kept me from a physical prison and brought me to redemption and freedom from addictions.

I can own responsibility for the choices I made back then. Bad choices.

So many times, we blame our upbringing or what someone taught us, and I can certainly claim those things. In the end, my choice of men didn't help raise my children well.

How much of it drifted into my sons? Into my daughters? Those questions haunt me if I let them. After many years, I learned to forgive myself and admit to my children that I made horrible mistakes, seeking their forgiveness.

All that is in the past. I can't change what I did or didn't do no more than I can change what my parents did or didn't do for me. No blame, no shame. We forget what lies behind and press forward in the race God called us to run. Because He forgave me, I can forgive myself and pray my children forgive me too.

I believe they have, and now, I share my story with a hope and prayer that the Lord uses it to help other mothers of inmates.

*"Your words are so powerful that they will kill or give life, and the talkative person will reap the consequences."*

— *King Solomon, Proverbs 18:21 (TPT)*

# Chapter 2 ~ Negative Heard—Negative Learned

During childhood, I was always told, "You gonna be like yo' daddy."

Hearing those words doesn't always represent negativity. In my case, they did. For a child with an absent father who kept more than one woman at a time, who abused those women and lived a lifestyle involved with illegal activity, those words didn't come as a compliment.

Despite his absence from most of my life, I still loved him, wanted to know him. I longed to feel his love. I never did, though. When I heard those words spoken over me, they didn't leave me with positive feelings.

Words have power—the capability to generate life or ability to produce death.

In normal families, children often want to grow up like mom or dad. Little girls care for baby dolls, using the same words they hear. They don tiny aprons and cook on pretend stoves. Little boys make every step their daddy takes, doing the things he does. Natural, normal learning for children to mimic parents.

Yet when we don't model good choices, they still grow up following in our footsteps. Even when they don't want to be like mom or dad, they end up with many of the tendencies we taught them intentionally or not.

To say, "You're just like your daddy," or "You act like your mama" may be the most negative thing you say to your children—especially if that parent doesn't show love and good judgement toward the child or life.

I must admit I repeated my mama's mistake. I told my children the same thing, even though they weren't around their daddy and knew little about him. I regret speaking those words over them now, and I would change it if possible. Instead, I confessed to them and apologized.

I knew a man whose family said they would rather see him locked up than covered up. Their sentiments and the accompanying emotions became my feelings just from hearing them speak those words. Not wanting to bury my children like we did my brother, I didn't care if they got picked up for illegal activity. At least they stayed alive.

I also knew young dudes that went to a boys' home as teens. I never knew what that was about or how their parents felt about dealing with it. For me, it was easy. I believed my sons were safer locked up than on the streets.

Of course, back then, I had a people addiction. I always followed other people's rules and regulations, doing my best to please everyone surrounding me. Trying to keep everyone else happy, I couldn't follow my rules or the ones I knew God put in place for me and my children to live a godly, happy life.

Unfortunately, not all those people wanted the best for us. They didn't truly care about me or my kids, and what they said or thought didn't always have positive outcomes. Addicted to pleasing others, I didn't weigh the words they spoke as negative or positive, but went along, carried by the wind of making everyone happy with me. That resulted in conflicting viewpoints and mixed advice which helped no one.

I've kicked it with a dude during my younger years. In prison, he asked during a phone conversation, "Have you wrote me? Have you put money on my book?"

His arrogant, demanding nature made me cower. "No," came out weak, knowing I didn't please him.

I could hear the astonishment in his voice. "You in the free world, with all the money, steaks."

> Words have power—the capability to generate life or ability to produce death.

He obviously didn't know me all that well. I barely scrimped by to pay bills and buy hamburger meat. The irony of it angered me. "I'm not free. You're in the free world. Everything in prison is free. Free lights, three, free square meals a day." I took a deep breath and pushed forward. "I might not be what you want, but you in the free world."

Of course, my commitment to him burned strong. I promised to put money up for him, buy his clothes and a car when they released him. Expecting him to marry me when he got released, that never happened. Just a female he used to get up on his feet, I loved him—he didn't love me.

For some unexplainable reason, I always wanted my children to have what I didn't— both parents in the same home. Didn't matter if one or both of us might cause my children to go down a wrong path. They needed a daddy, I thought. And if I had to sacrifice myself, I'd do it. If I had to put a man above their needs for a time, so be it.

From my mother and other women in my life, I came to believe you took care of a man to earn his love. If he beat you, that meant he loved you. To make matters worse, I hated being alone. More than my kids needed a daddy, I needed a man to feel whole. Warped view, I know now.

I learned I couldn't expect someone to love me if I didn't love myself or if he didn't love himself. The men I chose or wanted to choose had a selfish streak that ran for miles, but it didn't come from self-love. That selfishness came from self-indulgence, self-preservation, laziness and self-everything but true self-love.

I was a settler sista. I settled for anything and anybody. As I reflect on those years, I honestly didn't realize it didn't just affect me. Trust me, it affected me in some serious ways. But my willingness to settle also affected my children.

It had nothing to do with them. Back then, my selfish streak ran almost as many miles as that of most dudes I was with. I wanted what I believed good for my children, not realizing I gave them the worst possible role models.

I must admit, every time I met a dude, I welcomed him into my life and that of my kids without knowing much about him. In that state, I still told my kids to call him daddy.

Invariably, the dude only came around and played daddy when he needed to use me for sex, money, a place to stay. My self-esteem plummeted super low, although I didn't realize it at all.

After all my childhood sadness and terrible memories, I always said, "Pay close attention to children when they try to tell you something."

Mine kept trying to tell me something, and I didn't listen or believe the message they had for me. At least not until I became a mother of inmates. Then I heard what my babies tried to tell me over so many years.

No excuse, but hurt people tend to hurt other people. We never intend it, but we do it all the same. Unfortunately, the ones we seem to hurt most are the innocent children God gave us to protect and teach His ways.

I heard negative words in my life, learned them and embedded them in my soul. Without realizing it, I also taught my children some negative lessons and too often spoke negative words over them.

No more.

I strive to speak life over my children, to keep words positive and quit believing anything negative spoken over me. Sometimes, that means breaking ties with people and daring not to please them. From a process that took me years to understand, I pray others learn from me—especially my children.

> *"In a child's eyes, a mother is a goddess. She can be glorious or terrible, benevolent or filled with wrath, but she commands love either way. I am convinced that this is the greatest power in the universe."*
>
> — *N.K. Jemisin,* The Hundred Thousand Kingdoms

# *Chapter 3 ~*
# *I Didn't Realize*

As a child, sometimes I made the choice to do something I knew was wrong. Ironically, in those cases, I got whatever I wanted. When I behaved in ways I knew as right, I received nothing. It didn't take long for me to figure out that if I wanted something, behaving in negative ways got it for me. Negative reinforcement. Do bad, get a prize. Do good, get nothing. A bit warped, and I recognized that by the time my kids came along.

I considered myself flipping the script, refusing to do the same as Mama. My kids didn't receive gifts for misbehaving. I always told them, "Ain't no knowledge in Polo and Nikes or any material items."

I longed for my children to live right and not make the same decisions as I did. My feeble attempt to teach and reinforce good behavior over bad. It worked to some extent, I think. At least they knew I wouldn't go out and buy them some expensive item after they made a bad choice that got them in trouble with me or anyone else.

Still, I didn't realize I wasn't teaching them education. They needed to know good from bad, but they also needed basic education. At the time, I didn't have the knowledge to give them. If they learned in school, that gave them what they needed, but I couldn't help them with homework. If they didn't understand something their teachers taught, I couldn't make it clear to them. Although I eventually earned my high school diploma, in their younger years, my kids had to teach me some of those basic lessons.

Not that I was unintelligent. I just never had anyone show concern about whether I learned. My kids deserved better than that, but without the best education myself, I had no means to help them.

What my children learned from me, unfortunately, came from experiences I wish I could take back.

I didn't realize the damage to my children's emotions when I put men before them. Not wanting a life alone, trying to keep some dude happy, and hoping that dude acted like a daddy to my children. I messed up. When my paydays came, that guy-of-the-month might need some money. Too many times, one of his kids needed something. Sometimes, they looked like legitimate needs. Not my place to take care of it, I surrendered, daring not to disappoint that man.

Of course, I took care of him and his kid's business, often using my entire paycheck. When it came down to my own children or bills, I put them on the back burner. My kids went to school in old, worn-out jeans with holes when that meant poverty instead of being the "in" look. They might have worn tennis shoes with toes poking out the end or so tight they hurt their feet. I had to keep that father-figure for them, so I had to take care of him first. Looking back, I see how messed up that was.

When you don't love yourself, you take care of a man instead of him taking care of you. And in my case, I put someone else before my children only to watch him walk out of my life days later.

I didn't realize how kids could have laughed and talked about my children in school. It had to happen, because let's face it, all children have a mean streak. They have no problem making fun of others.

What my children learned from me, unfortunately, came from experiences I wish I could take back.

We never talked about it happening, so I never considered the possibility or realized my foolishness until much later in life.

Worse, at Christmas my kids didn't get anything. If we had a tree, it sat empty without a single present. A few months later, when income tax rolled around, and when I got a refund, I bought them gifts. That didn't make up for my kids knowing their friends and classmates got new toys and clothes in December. What did they say when everyone talked about the presents that they all got at Christmas? Again, those thoughts didn't enter my mind. I didn't realize how much damage I caused, the wounds I created that affected my little ones.

While I didn't realize the importance of my children, I counted the importance of others and their children—a mistake I hate to admit but must.

Some say ignorance is bliss, and perhaps that's true for the person who ignores reality. Whether I realized it, I hurt my children by showing more importance to others than I did for them.

We should help other people, and sharing from our blessings can teach our little ones a priceless lesson. But not if it makes them feel left out or unimportant to us as parents. Unknowingly, I taught my children they were less important than some loser who didn't stick around. I didn't feel that way. I loved my kids and more than anything wanted a daddy for them.

My mistake—believing money bought the love of a bad man who didn't deserve to be in my life or that of my children. God blessed me with four beautiful children, and I didn't always treat them as the precious treasures they are. Even imperfect, God entrusted them to me.

While I still don't believe I should reward them for behavior, good or bad, more than anything, I want them to know I count them more important than myself, my happiness and especially more than any man on this earth.

> *"My son, do not despise the chastening of the Lord, Nor be discouraged when you are rebuked by Him; For whom the Lord loves He chastens, And scourges every son whom He receives."*

*— Writer of Hebrews, 12:5-6*

# *Chapter 4 ~*
# *My Big Boy*

To respect his privacy, we'll call my firstborn Big Boy.

My mama's oldest grandson arrived during a messed-up time in my life. Before his birth, I lived a street life on drugs, prostituting, etc. If I could say getting pregnant stopped all that, perhaps my story might read differently. It didn't. The day I gave birth, my street life continued as strong as ever, pulling me away from him into the arms of addictions. Mama took him over as if he belonged to her instead of me. I had no objections.

You can't run the streets with a baby in your arms.

I never knew how to be a mother to him. Mama didn't treat him like she did me. Without a good role model, though, I didn't know how to take care of a baby. Honestly, caught up in my lifestyle, leaving him with Mama made the most sense. If she treated him better than she did me, he'd be fine with her.

Of course, I always saw how others treated their children. I tried to be a copycat and make an attempt at motherhood. Conflicting methods confused me. How could I make sense of the proper way to mother a child?

I watched a lot of people on drugs. They abused their kids verbally, physically, mentally and emotionally. Nothing kept them from hurting those children. I even knew some people who sold their children for drugs. They seemed to have no remorse, no concern with what the buyer wanted to do with those kids.

No one had to tell me not to follow those

people. Even in my drug-crazed mind, I knew better than that. The verbal abuse I suffered, watching my mama take beatings—I sensed that didn't show love to anyone. No matter what people said, I didn't want to treat my kids like that. And selling a baby? I might have been strung out, but I couldn't do that. Besides, Mama would've beaten me for that—and rightly so.

Well, maybe I should admit to a degree of verbal abuse. I learned that from the best, and the generational curses from my ancestors wanted to live for another generation. Because I didn't understand the power of words back then, I spoke things that didn't build up my children, but tore them down. I certainly whooped them when they needed it, but I didn't leave bruises or broken bones. Never.

> Still not knowing how to be the best mom, I knew enough to at least try to protect him.

While some of those days blur in my memory, I see Big Boy as a baby. I was smoking crack cocaine and didn't care if he ate. It was all about my dope. Admitting that pains me now. In the throes of addiction, a mother doesn't take care of anyone or anything but the driving ache of the next fix.

Big Boy got deathly ill, and we rushed him to the hospital with stomach problems. He had to have emergency surgery, requiring me to stay at the hospital for days while he recovered.

I couldn't.

That crack called me, begging me to leave and rush to it. I had to go get high and left my baby there alone. After a day or two, I went back to the hospital and stayed for a little while. Eventually, I left again, unable to fight the urge for more crack.

Then, I heard my so-called boyfriend at the time stole my stereo, sold it for dope. Pissed enough to choke him, I left the hospital again in search of the loser dude, forgetting that my baby needed me more than I needed a stereo.

After days of the back and forth for me, they released Big Boy from the hospital. That same day, we went to Mama's house. Of course, I didn't care what was going on.

We took off walking to the crack house.

Mama shouted at me. "Don't take that

baby nowhere."

She couldn't tell me nothing. Crack had control over me, blocking a mother's instinct to protect her baby just released from the hospital after surgery.

I don't care how many grandkids she had. Big Boy was Mama's baby. She watched out for him better than I did. Even when he was in school and wasn't on drugs, he stayed with her. I always wanted him to come live with me, but for some reason, his relationship with my mama was unending. At least until he got in trouble at school. Then Mama called me to come get him.

One time, they kicked him out of elementary school because he had a knife. He ended up kicked out of school altogether later. I had to enroll him in an alternative school. Trust me, it wasn't the first time. Two, three times, maybe more, I had to enroll him in alternative school or in juvenile detention. Mama loved having him at her house, but she kept calling when he ended up in trouble.

The call always came. "A mother is supposed to always be there for her children."

"Mama, why do you only call me to come get him when he gets in trouble? Then when the trouble is over, you want him back with you."

She didn't have much of an answer for that.

Another time, he hadn't been going to school, and I got the call. At times, when I got off work, I went to Mama's house. I found Big Boy, still fast asleep. I made him get up and go to school. He didn't like that much, but mothers make their kids go to school.

Other times, I pulled up and ran his friends away from the house—not the good kind of friends to keep him straight, but the ones that caused trouble and pulled him into it. He didn't need those friends. Still not knowing how to be the best mom, I knew enough to at least try to protect him. By that time, I no longer used drugs, hoping and praying my kids didn't get mixed up in them.

One Saturday, when I got home from work, I received a phone call. Big Boy got shot.

Memories of my brother whirled in me like a massive tornado, swirling, twisting, terrifying me as I waited for words I prayed didn't come. I knew only that he got shot. No details. No assurance of his condition. The breath left my chest, my heart squeezed by fear. I rushed to the hospital.

He didn't die. He shot himself in the foot. Of all the crazy things. Mad and relieved at the same time, the next revelation broke my heart.

The doctor planned to do emergency surgery but couldn't. Big Boy had drugs in his system.

Embarrassed and speechless, I stared at the doctor. No way. He always swore to me he didn't use dope.

The truth jumped out, again stealing my breath and tightening my chest. I always knew girls to lie about drugs and everything. But not boys. I never knew boys to lie until I found out he did. Again, the generational inheritance traveled from me to him. My son lied, just like I used to lie.

Around the age of 18, Big Boy began all his state jail and prison sentences. He picked me up from work one time, and the police arrested both of us for misdemeanors. I had no clue my son could get me in trouble.

Yes, it's difficult being a mother of inmates. Much like me in the years of addiction, he didn't care who he affected by his actions. Like me, he has to learn those consequences.

Big Boy's home now, and I'm thankful. Before he was released, I told him he could parole to my house. Then all of a sudden, I started feeling uncomfortable about the situation. I didn't know where those feelings originated and couldn't express all of what I felt. So, I prayed, telling God if it wasn't meant for him to parole at my house, please let him go somewhere else. He didn't.

I resented Big Boy because he had a better relationship with my mama than he did with me, and better than what I had with her. I found myself gossiping and complaining about my son, but he didn't have a problem I did. Unforgiveness crept back into my life, although I didn't yet see it.

I talked to the parole officer, asking them if Big Boy could go elsewhere. They told me they couldn't do it. He had to live with me.

Laughing behind the hurt and frustration, I went on that way for a while. All the mixed emotions toying with my spirit and creating unrest in me.

One night after work, I cried out to God in prayer only to get silence in return. Then, the next morning, God exposed me to myself. I've known hatred and unforgiveness, but I never thought I had it toward my child. The revelation undid me.

I prayed, "Lord, teach me how to forgive Big Boy."

After that, I went to my son and confessed my faults, asking him to forgive me. He did. More importantly, God forgave me and I forgave myself.

God has given us a new relationship. We knew of each other before that day, but we never knew each other. Now we laugh, we talk, pray, and we learned how to respect each other.

Three days after his release from prison, God blessed him with a job. I see changes in him.

I always said, "I'm tired, I ain't going to visit. Can't nobody parole to my house."

Scared at first, now I thank God for unity and my self-exposure. Big Boy also encouraged me to be an inspiration to his little brother, Baby Boy, while he remains incarcerated. With God's help, I'm trying my best.

"People pay for what they do, and still more for what they have allowed themselves to become. And they pay for it very simply; by the lives they lead."

— James Baldwin

## Chapter 5 ~ My Baby Boy

When Baby Boy came along, I still lived the street life of an addict.

A pregnant crack addict tends to have a big problem—her baby ends up having that same addiction through its mother's habit. Baby Boy entered the world addicted to drugs. What a trip listening to CPS (child protective services) telling me he was going to be a slow learner and malnourished. His life didn't begin as a picnic.

Over the years, he proved them wrong. It didn't turn out the way they predicted. He learned like any normal child, without a hint of any learning disabilities. He ate well and thrived in spite of me.

Although I got clean from crack cocaine, I had issues. I still didn't know how to be a mother. Never taught by my mother, I had no idea how to teach my children basic care for themselves. As I shared earlier, I always realized the need of others, but I didn't care or know the needs or worth for myself or my children.

Baby Boy excelled in school, very smart, but sadly, I never applauded him. Often, I went to the thrift store to purchase his shoes and clothes. He wore the same clothes every other day. When school started again each year, he didn't have new school clothes and shoes. Not just him, but none of my children.

I grieve over not providing for my children well, too often ignoring their needs, letting my so-called boo thangs come around. They took while my kids went back on hold. It hurts my heart to think of such a deep need for men that I let it rule over a mother's heart for her children.

Taught that mindset or not, I wish I could take it back, knowing I can't. I'm so grateful that God gave my children the mercy to forgive me and let it all go.

I never encouraged my kids to bathe. Like my mother before me, I told them, "Just get up, get ready for school." I didn't care what they wore either. Baby Boy pretty much had only one or two outfits at a time. Not even a pair of jeans with multiple shirts. I recall a pair of green pants and some maroon hiking boots when he was in elementary school. He wore them all the time. I never considered how he could have been getting teased and made fun of for wearing the same things repeatedly.

Baby Boy had a tender heart, with his feeling easily hurt. He ended up wounded because he needed school clothes. Instead of me buying school clothes for my son, I hosted a birthday party for another dude's child. I didn't have money to pay my

> Surrounded by emotional pain that cripples us, we don't necessarily want God to tell us He allowed it so we can help someone else.

bills in that instance. Not my finest moment.

When he still was in elementary school, phone calls from the school commenced. He got in trouble for one thing or another. Leaving work, I went up to school repeatedly. It involved all my kids since I didn't get paid for that time away from work.

I sometimes told my kids, "I had to miss work because of Baby Boy, so y'all gotta wait on gifts for Christmas."

Or wait on a birthday present, or wait for new clothes or shoes. It didn't help when I spent money on others before them anyway, and then brought home a smaller check. It never occurred to me that I caused some of the issues in his heart by opening him to the teasing.

Baby Boy started getting suspended from school. Eventually, he made it to Juvenile Probation, and that led to Juvenile Detention. One day, I found marijuana under his pillow. I didn't have a clue about his friends, who he hung with. I remember him asking if he could stay a night with his friends. Sometimes, I said no, but other times, I let him, not knowing anything about the parents at all. I later discovered these parents were using or selling drugs.

Of course, my focus was on some dude, not Baby Boy. In middle school, he played football. I didn't focus on him doing well or support him. I spent my time focused only on working and getting some dude's attention, even though he wasn't stuttin' me.

Baby eventually got a charge for theft. Angry and frustrated, I spoke negatively about him to the judge. I couldn't keep him out of trouble, and that old saying replayed in my head. Better locked up than covered up.

They released him a year later but sent him to a drug treatment center. Six months later, he spent nine months at a boy's home out of town. My heart hurt in an awful way because I couldn't keep my son out of trouble. With him out-of-town, I couldn't visit him easily either.

Eventually he was released with his GED in hand. After all that, I thought a change would come. I hoped he learned from all that time locked up and prayed he didn't repeat the same choices.

I wondered if Baby Boy saw me with all those thugs and drug dealers. He wanted what they had—big fancy cars, money and women. I'm not sure of Baby Boy's mindset, but that's how I felt. The material belongings he saw looked good, and their way of getting them seemed the easiest route.

I worked hard and barely made enough to live. Those dudes in my life, and others my kids saw, did little work and enjoyed a plush existence with more than enough materially.

In reality, that lifestyle held big rewards, but it also carried a giant risk and massive cost he didn't see. Prison and county jail sentences strip freedom. Those cars, money and women don't stick around while a man's gone.

Then the phone calls came from the county jails and state prison. When Big Boy got out, Baby Boy went in, and vice versa. Can you imagine these two brothers or me and all my children not being together for over four years? Not an easy feeling to imagine.

When Baby Boy was released from state prison, I connected him with a staffing agency. Yes, he started working. He stayed out of trouble and jail for a few years. I let myself relax for the first time in years. Finally. Maybe he changed, started walking on the right path, and life could be good for all of us.

Then I got a call. Baby Boy went to Federal Prison.

My heart shattered, agony piercing my soul. What would Baby Boy do every day, so far from home in another state? If allowed to visit, how could I find enough money to go?

The unbearable ache in my heart brought me to my knees and to prayer again.

Not overnight, but after a while, God spoke to me in the midst of pain. He told me this would be a ministry—not only local, but nationwide in the prisons.

God said, "Teresa, you had to go through what you went through to go tell others."

We don't want to hear that. Surrounded by emotional pain that cripples us, we don't necessarily want God to tell us He allowed it so we can help someone else. Yet knowing God intended to use for good what the enemy meant to destroy me and my children left me with hope.

The Bible says we are overcomers by the power of His blood and by the word of our testimonies.

As I meditated on these thoughts, He showed me how so many mothers lost their children due to death. Even though I get tired of being a mother of inmates, at least I can talk to and see my children. Some parents wish they could. Wish they had a chance to still reach their grown-up babies.

Sometimes, mine ended up incarcerated while others with them died. I realized God had a message in those thoughts, letting me know He got them covered and protected. Even when it looks the worst, there's always good amidst it all.

I told my children name-brand shoes and clothes didn't give them any knowledge, believing I was flippin' the script. Revelation scared me, as I understood my choices were no better than my mama's. I did the opposite of her and never rewarded my children or put them first.

They paid a heavy price for my mistakes, and I carry that pain with me.

Once again, God forgives. I pray my sons and daughters forgive my terrible misunderstanding of what was most important. And through God's grace, I forgive myself.

*"Parenthood...It's about guiding the next generation, and forgiving the last."*
— Peter Krause (Parenthood)

# Chapter 6 ~
# Parents, Check Yourself

Being a single mother of inmates was super stressful, more than overwhelming. One child incarcerated could break any mother. Two at the same time? If not for God, I couldn't bear it.

Over the course of my sons' incarcerations, holidays rolled around. Many mothers find it kinda hard to have all their children around during holidays. Others love having families all together, regardless of the extra work it involves. Either way, most mothers enjoy having their children together to celebrate any holiday, but I didn't have the option. When you have a child in the county jail, state or federal prison, they can't come home and spend time with family. It doesn't involve a choice. They simply can't.

I found myself complaining about missing work because I had to go to juvenile court. Multiple times I caught myself saying, "I ain't going to visit them, ain't putting no money on their books. I ain't writing them, and I sure ain't getting no house phone for them to call."

Those words came from a place of pain, anger and frustration. I needed to check myself.

Throughout my life, if a request or demand had something to do with a dude, I obeyed him without a thought or moment's hesitation. Letting him use me while imprisoned, I convinced myself that when he got out, we would be together. He would be a dad to my kids and marry me.

Umm, not so.

That dude (and more like him) used me to make his life more comfortable. When released, he was long gone and going about his business—until he got locked back up. Suddenly, he remembered me.

As time went on, I realized he wasn't for me, and he could only do what I allowed. I dumped that dude. Unfortunately, in my addiction to people pleasing, and my desire not to be alone, another dude stepped in that same hole. I repeated the pattern many times until I finally looked hard at my weaknesses and wounds. Once God healed me, I didn't need those dudes who only wanted to use me until I had nothing left to use.

Later, I realized why some people be in the streets selling drugs. On my end, I always worked, making sure this dude or that dude was ok with all he needed.

But what about my children?

Girls need their hair done, and boys need haircuts. They all need clothes. They see other children presentable, decent, but they're not. Eventually, they see how drug dealers get big money, nice fancy cars. Ironically, people on the streets speak highly of them. Bam! Regrettably, your children start following the negative choices of others.

You can't teach your children what you don't know. You can't love them as you should when you never received the right kind of love. When you learn where you messed up, though, you can change and share with your children where you went wrong so they can become better parents than you.

> While I regret my past, I learned to allow God to heal the shame, forgive me and teach me to forgive myself.

Being a parent, we not only have to moderate who our children have in their circle, but we must moderate who we let in our circle. Indirectly, anyone in our circles becomes part of their circles, sometimes causing more damage than we can imagine.

Demons look for a resting place. If a spirit lives in someone else, and you allow them into your circle and you're open, that spirit can rest in you. Unintentional, and sometimes unimaginable, it happens, and much of the time we never see the exchange until later.

When children are in school, and they are being bullied, nine times out of ten, the bullies endure bullying by others, either at school or home. Yes, siblings and even parents bully kids. Children repeat what happens to them. A lot of things can come from generational curses. Hidden secrets no one ever spoke about within their families.

Think about molesters that someone else molested. Abusers who often experienced abuse of themselves or watching as one parent abused the other. Drug users and alcoholics who grew up with one or both parents addicted.

As a mother of inmates, I admit I grew up with multiple issues. I was hated, maybe by my own parents. A lot of things I did to my children left me feeling that the trouble they got into was my fault. We don't want to admit that or even think it. However, when I check myself, I can't deny my mistakes.

Things I couldn't teach them, not knowing some of it myself. Issues with self-esteem, people pleasing and more. No excuses, but exploring these reasons helped me see how I affected my children in negative ways. While I regret my past, I learned to allow God to heal the shame, forgive me and teach me to forgive myself.

Holding regret and seeking forgiveness for the things you did in the past is pure anguish. During this process, I couldn't stop crying, my heart agonizing and wrestling with my mind. I didn't know what to do, but I continued to pray until breakthrough came. My children told me, "Mama, the past is the past. Don't hold on to stuff like that."

All this inside, years of holding unforgiveness for others—so painful. Imagine not being able to forgive yourself for the past. I lived there for a season. Then, I began encouraging myself, speaking the words, "I forgive me."

In the past lies my testimony, and maybe it can help someone else. I thank God I overcame it all.

As so much of this became clearer to me, I prayed and asked God to teach my children how to forgive me. I wanted to let His light shine through me so it could draw them unto Him. If they could see the changes in me, maybe I had hope for redemption in myself, and my sons and daughters.

I begin the difficult task of apologizing to my children, uncertain of how they might respond. Knowing I had to be painfully honest, I confessed to them that I haven't been the best parent. Then, I told them, "Whatever I did wrong, please forgive me." They had plenty of potential wounds to pick, and I knew at some point if they didn't forgive me, the generational curses would continue. More than anything, I wanted that to cease.

Enough.

The enemy had his season in my family, but I wanted to stop it from going forward. I wanted it to end so my grandbabies never knew the pain I endured and inflicted on their parents.

Baby Boy still got in trouble, but he didn't want me to know. Although he tried hiding the truth, I always found out.

Once he told me, "Don't stress, it's not your fault."

My life affected his, and I had to admit that, but he knew an important truth. At some point in life, each person must stop blaming someone else. What your mama or daddy did or didn't do affects you, but it only defines you if you allow it. Maturity means you quit blaming someone else and accept responsibility for what you did, how you reacted to the negative pieces of your past, and the poor choices you made regardless of whether you knew better.

I want to encourage all parents of inmates

to check yourself. And when you see errors in yourself, let God forgive you, ask others for forgiveness in the way it hurt them. Then, learn to forgive yourself.

Two wrongs don't make a right. Some children stole just to have nice clothes because their parents wouldn't or maybe couldn't buy them anything. Maybe they only had money for thrift store clothes, and didn't know a way out to do more. Sometimes, they simply lived selfishly, high on drugs or alcohol, or like me, trying to please people who didn't matter.

Unfortunately, children get caught and become inmates. And as mothers, we suffer the consequences, whether we contributed to their choices.

I had to learn not to do evil for evil. I must admit when someone did something to me, I told my boys, not realizing I influenced them. Trying to protect and avenge me, they got in trouble. Sometimes, I bragged and boasted about what and who my boys are. Not realizing their actions resulted from my words, and if they got into trouble, that was on me. I could be going about my business and stressed, but my sons needed to fix things for me.

So, who's fault would it be when they

ended up in trouble? Of course, mine.

Yes, indeed, I had to start checking myself and stop the foolishness and getting them involved with my issues. Again, I turned to prayer and read Matthew 5:44. "But I say to you, love your enemies, bless those who curse you, do good to those who hate you, and pray for those who spitefully use you and persecute you."

Psalms 37 also taught me not to fret over evildoers, to do good myself and trust God to take care of those who hurt me. If I went to God with these issues instead of my sons, left it with Him, I could count on Him to take care of everything without causing more trouble for Big Boy and Baby Boy.

I had another issue—talking too much. Perhaps it stemmed from that old spirit of gossiping I struggled with for years. I learned it from my mother, but God convicted me of it. Although I asked God to heal me from it, I caught myself continuing to share things with others who had no business knowing all the details of mine or my children's lives.

As soon as one of my babies did wrong, everyone knew everything. It didn't come from other people sharing those tidbits, but from me.

God convicted me and made me realize they kept a lot of secrets from me. While they didn't want to hurt me, they also didn't appreciate the way I told so many people all about them. I told too much information to too many people—some who knew my sons, but some who never met them.

Imagine your child looking up to someone else because they can't trust their parents, and the other person ends up being a bad mentor. Once again, I had to check myself. How could I expect my babies to listen only because I'm their mama? Telling them how to do right while I spread all manner of negativity?

Consider the people I told my problems to if they had issues. They couldn't trust sharing anything with me because I constantly told other people's business. Oh, that nasty gossiping spirit, rising to the surface, hiding in the pretense of sharing the need for prayer even. Going to a trusted confidant for prayer support helps, but spreading gossip never helps anyone.

Once God exposed these issues to me, I surrendered the nasty habit to God. Growing up, I watched my mama gossiping on the phone every morning before she went to work, and I started doing the same thing. Even as a child, I called one of my classmates.

Her mom answered the phone and said, "Here go gossiping Teresa."

I didn't understand what she meant then, but when God brought up this memory, I got it. I had a gossiping and complaining spirit in me which was a generational curse. The years of spreading negativity didn't only shape me, it impacted my children.

When God revealed these things, I didn't want to let go of them. Almost impossible to give up, I grew so comfortable in the same spot and repeated habits of gossiping and complaining. In many ways, it gave me the attention I craved too. For God to take me to the next level, I had to surrender all that trash molded in me. I wanted more of what God planned for me, so I gave it to Him, trusting that He had the power to remove those spirits and replace them with positivity.

How could I encourage others to do positive when I continued walking in so much negativity and sharing the worst parts of others with everyone? I couldn't, and only God could teach me to stop.

Age and a person's relationship have nothing to do with maturity. A five-year-old can have far more wisdom and maturity than some in their 50s or older. Age doesn't guarantee maturity. Some never want to grow up and accept the responsibility for wrongs they did in the past. Nor do they want to change.

Until we decide to make things right, we won't mature. Who wants to remain childish in the most important things? Not me. Admitting many of these things to myself first, then agreeing with God, receiving His forgiveness, and then seeking it from others, I began a process of reaching maturity.

While I remain far from perfect, I know I'm at a higher place and more mature than ever before. In this place, I can become more of what my children need from me even as adults.

From one parent to another, I encourage you to check yourself. Honestly, openly check your heart. Admit any issues hiding inside and deal with them as God directs.

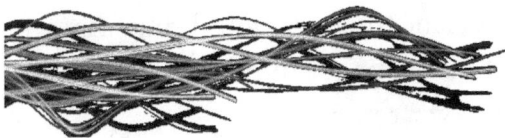

*"And don't allow yourselves to be weary in planting good seeds, for the season of reaping the wonderful harvest you've planted is coming!"*
— *The Apostle Paul, Galatians 6:9 (TPT)*

# Chapter 7 ~
# Then and Now

What a difference—then and now. Over decades of living and learning, I can say my life looks nothing like did during the early years with my babies. All adults now, they remain my babies.

I birthed four children. Not all of them became inmates, and I thank God for that. Two of them broke laws and became inmates.

One remains incarcerated, and I pray that when released, I can support him and help him start fresh and never return.

I can admit my wrong, how I failed with all four of my children. I couldn't raise them to be perfect because I wasn't perfect. For a good part of my life, I didn't practice the right way to live, so only by God's grace did two of them stay out of trouble.

Of course, I taught them how to clean up, to be respectful. When I learned these things, I wanted my kids to do them better than I ever did.

Even before I came to know Jesus on a personal level, I talked to them about God. During times in my life, I wondered if He existed or cared about me, but I wanted my children to know about God.

Still, I was smoking cigarettes, gossiping, complaining, having sex outside marriage, and I wasn't concerned about myself or my children. The badness in me went further even though I didn't realize it, or maybe I didn't truly care. My children caught the blows of the things I did.

With my oldest daughter, I left her with people I knew nothing about, allowing the possibility of terrible things. The enemy reminds me of the past and how much my daughters might have suffered because of my poor choices.

I'm so grateful they don't hold it against me now, and that both stayed out of prison. They could very well have followed the same path as their brothers. They didn't, which proves we can make better decisions than our parents ever did.

Life hands families the same situations. God gave my girls the wisdom to take the more difficult way to live, and I thank Him so much.

Sometimes, I needed food or gas, knowing my babies didn't have jobs. Working at a job, I had the nerve to ask them for money. They cared about me, wanting to take care of my needs. How crazy was that after I failed them so many times?

In addition, I tended to attempt getting my kids involved if I had issues with some guy. I wanted somebody taking up for me, and that's not the responsibility of a child at any age. I vented so many of my problems to them without considering how they might react.

God showed me that when I did that, I encouraged them to get fast money, even if it meant doing something illegal. Again, I had to surrender to God. The process of seeking His forgiveness, asking my kids for forgiveness and then forgiving myself took so much energy. But I had to do it.

How could I encourage them to do wrong after God gave me this revelation? Once I surrendered to God, I couldn't accept knowing I unwittingly caused them to do wrong at the same time I expected them to live right. I no longer could claim ignorance, and with God's help, I quit asking them to provide for me.

Now, I don't like telling people what I got going on. I don't want anyone getting into trouble because of my problems. I realize my issues with someone else has nothing to do with the next person. If I need prayer support or perspective because I'm hurting, I trust a few close friends and turn to them, not expecting them to deliver me, but to listen and counsel me wisely.

I had a lot of regret over my sons' incarceration, knowing some of it was my fault. I mentally beat myself up for a lot of the things I did, and found it challenging to forgive myself. Although they don't blame me, I still regret what they went through.

I keep telling them, "As long as you're living, you're never too old to do anything good you want to do."

I'm grateful to be here, just to let them know how much I love them. I pray constantly that God will remove all

I can admit my wrong, how I failed with all four of my children. I couldn't raise them to be perfect because I wasn't perfect.

negative people from their lives, so they will not continue to get in trouble. No more jails, no more prison for them. And I asked God to teach me how to be a better parent for all four of my babies. Our relationship is not perfect, but it's way better than before.

I once watched the movie *Losing Isaiah*. The story in that movie ripped at my heart, leaving me filled with regret over my addiction to smoking crack. I cried over my children and a lot of things I did. If I never did this stuff, maybe my children wouldn't have ended up in this predicament—in and out of prison, in and out of juvenile detention.

As I considered these thoughts, the ache in

my heart tore at me. If I could go back and change my past, I wouldn't hesitate for the sake of my kids.

That was then. Once I began to surrender all my issues to God, He spoke about my ministry's name—Hurt-Broken-Now Healed and Delivered Ministries. Feeding the homeless and hosting youth extravaganzas only touched the surface of His plan.

What touched me the most is when God said, "Whatever seed you sow that's what fruit you will produce."

Eventually, I started hosting job fairs for people with criminal backgrounds. I reached a point where I saw people with a job making $2 an hour. Not necessarily enough to live, but being a productive member of society can keep kids and adults from getting in trouble and going back to prison.

This is something I would like to encourage everyone, even if you've never been to jail or prison. Never let your past hinder you from moving forward. There's no excuse to remain stuck in a lesser place, because God's got your back.

Sometimes it doesn't feel that way. During trials and unbearable circumstances, you may not see His hand. Like I did at one time in my life, you may think He hates you. If I learned anything up to this point in life, I know undoubtedly, that isn't true. He allows situations in our lives to teach us lessons, and whether we like it, sometimes, He uses life to prepare us for ministering to others.

Trust that God has your best interest at heart, and Jesus came so we can enjoy an abundant life. The enemy wants to steal, kill and destroy God's chosen people, and he tries so hard to do exactly that. We can overcome and lead others into God's light when we choose to surrender it all to Him.

"Brethren, I do not count myself to have apprehended; but one thing I do, forgetting those things which are behind and reaching forward to those things which are ahead, I press toward the goal for the prize of the upward call of God in Christ Jesus." Philippians 3:13-14

Keep moving forward.

The best choice I made? Telling all my children the truth. "I haven't been the best parent to you. If I did anything to you (and I know in my heart I did), please forgive me." Then, I tell them repeatedly, "I love you."

After I beat myself up for the choices I made, I put down that big stick, and I forgive myself, fully assured that if God can forgive me, I can too.

I have been crucified with Christ;
it is no longer I who live, but
Christ lives in me; and
the life which I now live in the
flesh I live by faith in the Son of
God, who loved me and gave
Himself for me.
(Galatians 2:20)

# *About the Author*

Founder and CEO of Hurt, Broken, Now Healed and Delivered Ministries, Teresa Tarpley released her first book in 2016, *HeartBroken: Now Healed and Delivered.* In ministering to other people, Teresa focuses on those coming out of addiction and striving to live a new life with Jesus as their guide.

In 2017, Teresa became a radio talk show host of *Straight Up Radio Talk Show.* Based on her life story, she launched the stage play *I am Beautiful,* as the executive producer. Teresa also played a part in the stage play, which opened doors for several minor roles in movies. She became a certified actress.

Recognized for the best stage play executive producer during 2019 Phoenix, Arizona Teresa enjoys acting with hopes that each role she plays ministers to someone. In addition, she shares her testimony whenever the opportunity arises.

She released a follow-up to her story in 2021 with *Why Y'all Treat Me So Bad?* As a mother with an incarcerated son, Teresa felt compelled to write in her transparent style and now has released *Mother of Inmates* as her third book. Although written from the perspective of a mother with sons, it applies to women with daughters equally, and fathers can benefit from what she shares too.

All her books are available at discounted prices for bulk purchases, sales promotions, fund-raising events or for educational purchases.

For more information about the author, to obtain special pricing or to schedule Teresa as a speaker for your event, please contact Teresa Tarpley by phone or email.

PO Box 50162
Fort Worth, TX 76105
(817) 210-7517
Email: minister.ttarpley@yahoo.com

# *About Radical Women*

Owner of Radical Women, Lisa Bell, lives in Granbury, Texas where she works as an editor for NOW Magazines, LLC, covering two of nine markets. She provides freelance editing of all types (including developmental editing) and strives to guide and assist writers in publishing their stories independently or with traditional publishers. Whether fiction or non-fiction, Lisa has experience and knowledge to make a good story great.

Lisa also serves as a coach for two writing groups under the name of Radical Writers. She strives to teach writers the skills of writing so their work becomes the best they can achieve. Through writing groups, individual coaching, editing and more, she takes pride in finished products that rival any book regardless of the publisher.

Lisa has published hundreds of articles and multiple books. You can learn more about Lisa, see her works in progress, or contact her by visiting
www.bylisabell.com.
(817) 269-9066
lisabell@bylisabell.com

# *Other Books by Teresa Tarpley*

❖    *HeartBroken: Now Healed and Delivered*

Published March 28, 2016
Radical Women
978-0692583739

❖    *Why Y'all Treat Me So Bad?*

Published June 14, 2021
Radical Women
978-1734039832

** Available in Kindle and Print versions at
www.amazon.com and other retailers. **

There's no excuse not to move
forward because God's got my back.
~Teresa Tarpley

www.ingramcontent.com/pod-product-compliance
Lightning Source LLC
Chambersburg PA
CBHW061157040426
42445CB00013B/1707